Extremely WEIRD

MICRO MONSTERS

Text by Sarah Lovett

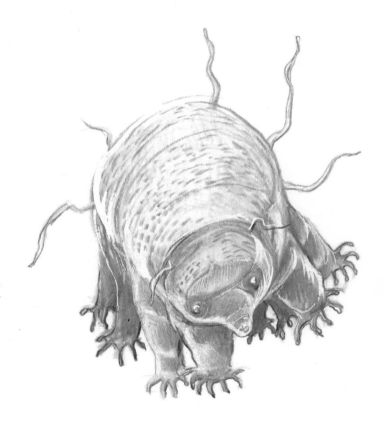

John Muir Publications
Santa Fe, New Mexico

SPECIAL THANKS to Gene Harrell, Biology Consultant, Santa Fe, New Mexico

John Muir Publications, P.O. Box 613, Santa Fe, NM 87504
Copyright © 1993 by John Muir Publications
All rights reserved.
Printed in the United States of America

Second edition. First printing August 1996

Library of Congress Cataloging-in-Publication Data
Lovett, Sarah, 1953–
   Micro monsters / text by Sarah Lovett;
[illustrations, Mary Sundstrom, Beth Evans]. — 2nd ed.
      p.   cm. — (Extremely weird)
   Includes index.
   Summary: Photographs and drawings introduce twenty
unusual microscopic organisms, including the red blood cell,
influenza virus, head louse, and red spider mite.
   ISBN 1-56261-293-X (pbk.)
   1. Microorganisms—Juvenile literature. [1. Microoganisms.
2. Microbiology.] I. Sundstrom, Mary, ill.   II. Evans, Beth, ill.
III. Title. IV. Series: Lovett, Sarah, 1953 – Extremely weird
QR57.L685   1996
595—dc20   96-14766
                           CIP
                           AC

Extremely Weird Logo Art: Peter Aschwanden
Illustrations: Mary Sundstrom, Beth Evans
Design: Sally Blakemore
Printer: Guynes Lithographers

Distributed to the book trade by
Publishers Group West
Emeryville, California

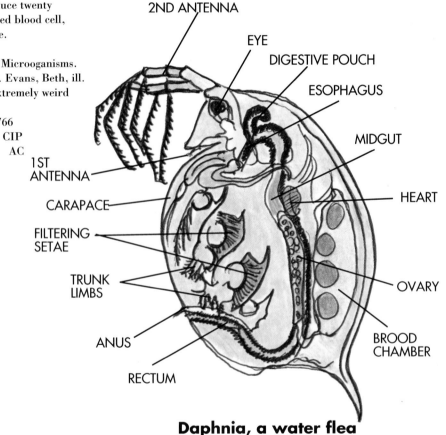

Daphnia, a water flea

2ND ANTENNA
EYE
DIGESTIVE POUCH
ESOPHAGUS
MIDGUT
HEART
1ST ANTENNA
CARAPACE
FILTERING SETAE
TRUNK LIMBS
ANUS
RECTUM
OVARY
BROOD CHAMBER

Cover photo: HUMAN HEAD LOUSE (*Pidiculus humanus capitis*)
Human head lice are wingless insects that feed on human
blood sucked from the scalp.
Cover photo courtesy © SPL/Custom Medical Stock Photo

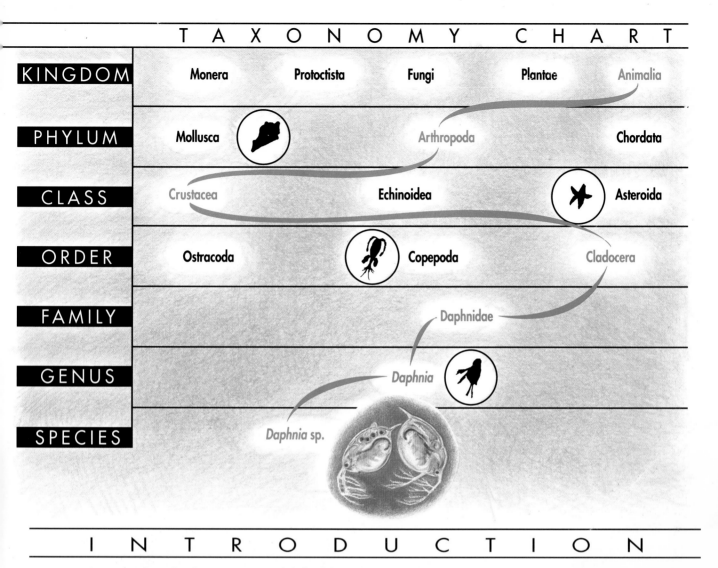

KINGDOM	Monera	Protoctista	Fungi	Plantae	Animalia
PHYLUM	Mollusca		Arthropoda		Chordata
CLASS	Crustacea		Echinoidea		Asteroida
ORDER	Ostracoda		Copepoda		Cladocera
FAMILY			Daphnidae		
GENUS			Daphnia		
SPECIES	Daphnia sp.				

I N T R O D U C T I O N

Do you remember the last time you felt lonely? The next time you think you're all alone, think again. Even if your room *looks* empty, you've got company. Millions of living critters are hidden in places you never thought to look: inside your intestines and your vacuum cleaner, for instance, and under your mattress, around your eyelashes, and even in your blood and the air you breathe. Just because you can't see them doesn't mean they're not there.

The micro monsters (microorganisms) in this book can be grouped together because they are all extremely difficult (or impossible) to see without the aid of a microscope. They're all living, of course! Well, all except the influenza virus on page 8. Scientists still disagree on whether a virus is a simple form of life or just a complex molecule, which is a stable group of atoms and electrons.

Some of these micro monsters are "monstrous" because they cause harm to other living things. Others only look like monsters when they are magnified fifty or a hundred times. Many of the photos in this book have been taken with the aid of a scanning electron microscope (SEM).

All scientists use one system to keep track of the millions of animal and plant species on Earth. That system is called taxonomy, and it starts with the five main (or broadest) groups of all living things, the kingdoms. (The micro monsters in this book represent all five scientific kingdoms.) Taxonomy then divides those into the next groups down—phylum, then class, order, family, genus, and, finally, species. Members of a species look similar, and they can reproduce with each other.

For an example of how taxonomy works, follow the highlighted lines above to see how the daphnia (*Daphnia* sp.) is classified. In this book, the taxonomic scientific name of each creature is listed next to the common name. In a few cases, only the scientific family or species name is used. Remember, cells do not have taxonomic names, but unicellular (single-celled) organisms do.

Turn to the glossarized index if you're looking for a specific micro monster, or for special information (where bacteria live, for instance), or for the definition of a word you don't understand.

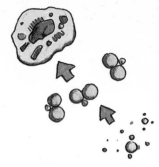

INFLUENZA VIRUS

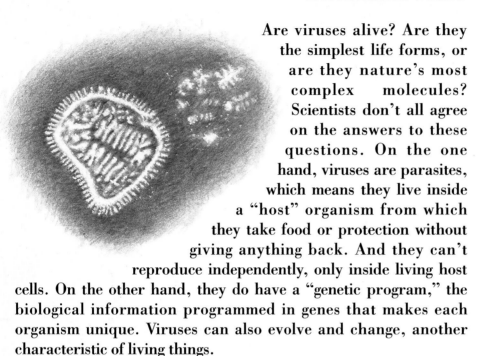

Are viruses alive? Are they the simplest life forms, or are they nature's most complex molecules? Scientists don't all agree on the answers to these questions. On the one hand, viruses are parasites, which means they live inside a "host" organism from which they take food or protection without giving anything back. And they can't reproduce independently, only inside living host cells. On the other hand, they do have a "genetic program," the biological information programmed in genes that makes each organism unique. Viruses can also evolve and change, another characteristic of living things.

But even if viruses are not living, they have a great impact on the biosphere. Many viruses cause disease, some in epidemic proportions. (An epidemic is a disease that spreads rapidly.) Both the common cold and the flu are caused by a virus.

Although the influenza virus pictured at right looks like a happy face, it can make humans very sick. Influenza viruses cause diseases such as Spanish, Asian, and Hong Kong flu. These flus occur all over the world, and they usually recur every ten to forty years because the virus changes its genetic program and human memory cells (remember the lymphocyte?) don't recognize it.

Viruses are sometimes called the "wheels of evolution" because they take pieces of one organism's genetic program and give it to another completely different organism. This helps to create biodiversity, the astounding variety of living things on our planet.

In 1984, researchers discovered that AIDS, which stands for Acquired Immune Deficiency Syndrome, is caused by a virus they named HIV. AIDS has become such a big epidemic many researchers now call it a pandemic. (*Pan* is Latin for *all*.) A pandemic has the potential to spread to every continent on the globe. HIV mutates (changes its genetic program) faster than any other virus ever studied by scientists.

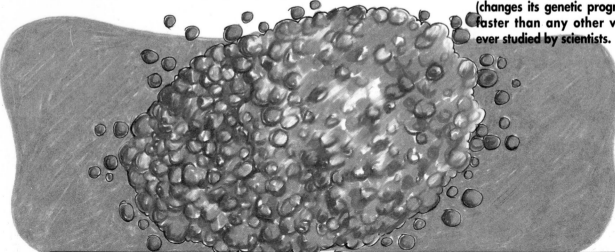

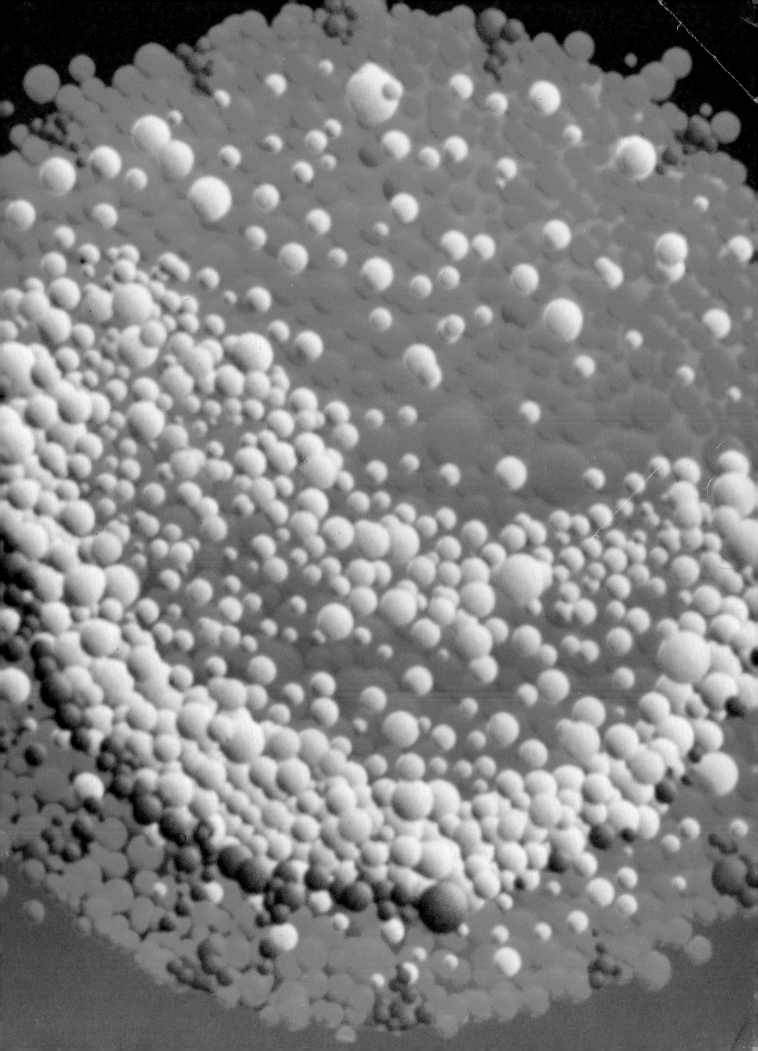

BACTERIA (*Proteus mirabilis*)

Proteus mirabilis is a species of bacteria that plays an important role in microbial ecology because it helps decompose, or break down, organic matter so it can be reused as fertilizer by plants. The bacterium moves by waving its numerous flagella, threadlike extensions of its cell.

Proteus mirabilis lives in polluted waters and in manure, garden soil, and the feces of animals. It is also found in the intestines of some healthy humans, where it aids in the formation of urine.

But humans are mostly concerned with *Proteus* because it causes serious infections and can be resistant to some types of antibiotics. So, is this bacterium a "good guy" or a "bad guy"? When we judge another living organism as helpful or harmful, we are usually concerned with its direct impact on us. But every living thing is part of the web of life, and it's important to look at how each organism helps to maintain the biological and ecological balance on Earth.

Proteus was so-named by a scientist in the late 1800s because it reminded him of Proteus, the god in Greek mythology who was able to take different shapes.

How many flagella can you count at right?

Answer: Each *Proteus* has exactly 176 flagella.

Bacteria are the simplest types of living cells. They are also one of the most successful life forms on Earth.

Photo, facing page © SPL/Custom Medical Stock Photo

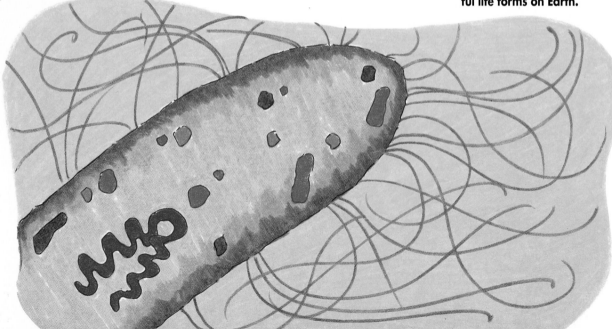

MICRO MONSTERS

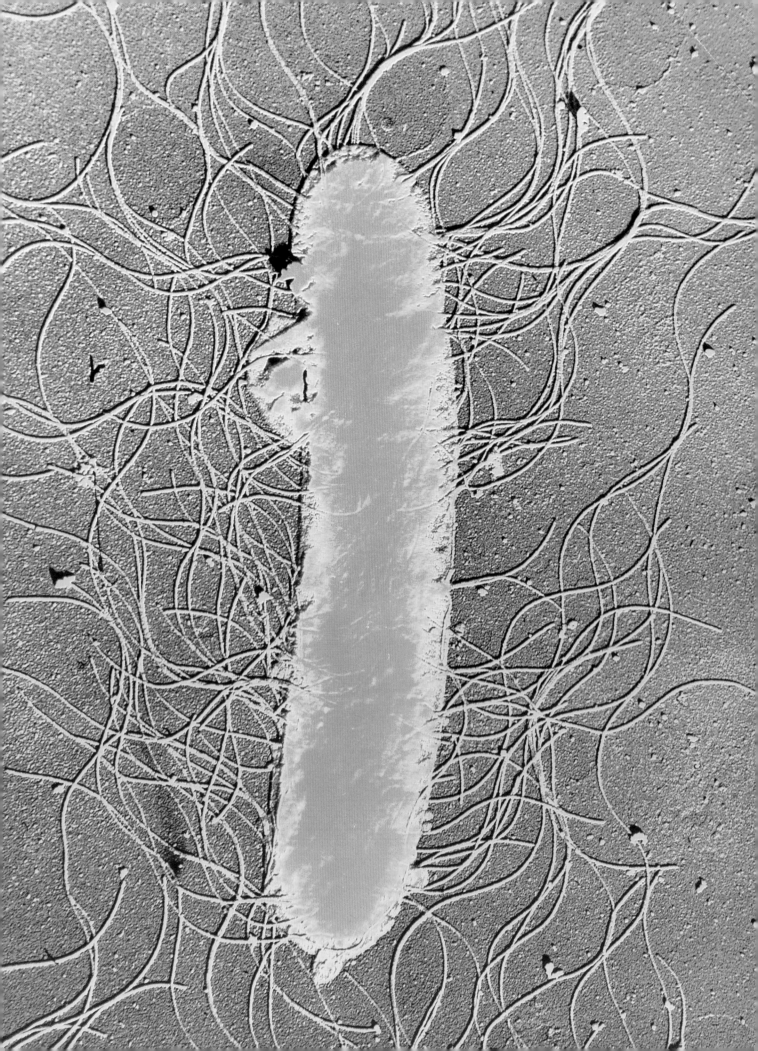

HUMAN HEAD LOUSE (*Pediculus humanus capitis*)

The human head louse belongs to a family of true (or sucking) lice that live and feed only on human primates. Besides the human head louse, humans also play host to the body louse (*Pediculus humanus corporis*). Other primates, such as chimpanzees and gorillas, host their own members of this true louse family.

Primate lice are part of a recent family in evolutionary terms. They are developing only as quickly as their hosts—we primates—allow them to. As we evolve and change, so do they.

True lice feed on blood that they draw from their host with their piercing and sucking mouthparts. They also need the vitamins they receive from the bacteria living inside their own minuscule bodies—which means there are parasites inside parasites. While the lice gain nutritional benefits, the bacteria live and breed inside their lice hosts. In fact, new generations of bacteria are transmitted to new generations of lice through the host eggs. In biology, this type of mutually beneficial living arrangement is known as symbiosis or mutualism.

While human head lice live in hair, human body lice survive on clothing or bedding and jewelry and only climb onto the skin to move around.

Fleas (relatives of lice) are incredible athletes. A member of one tropical species can average one jump per second for as long as 72 hours if it is excited by nearby fleas.

Photo, facing page, Animals Animals © Alastair MacEwen

BEEF TAPEWORM (*Taenia saginata*)

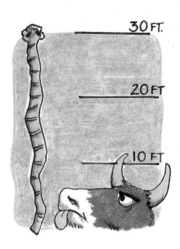

A single tapeworm can live for 30 to 35 years! It's pear-shaped head is about 1 to 2 millimeters in diameter and it may reach a length of 10 meters (over 30 feet).

Tapeworms are parasites, and most have hooks and suckers on their head, the better to attach themselves to someone else. Although beef tapeworms have four egg-shaped suckers, they are called "weaponless tapeworms" because they sport no ring of hooks.

Young beef tapeworms reside inside the fat and muscle tissue of cattle, African zebus, and buffalo. How do they get there? By accident, when cattle and other large herbivores eat the tapeworm eggs in their food. Each egg envelope contains a hooked larva. When the cow's intestinal juices dissolve the envelope, the larva burrows freely through the intestines to reach the host's blood system. There it develops into a "bladder worm" that carries the head of a new tapeworm within it. But the tapeworm will never reach maturity unless it finds a new host—a person!

When people eat very rare meat or raw meat, they may also be eating a tapeworm. Once inside a human host, the ribbon of new reproductive organs located behind a tapeworm's head continues to grow. Sections of the ribbon separate into segments containing both male and female sex organs. Tapeworms are known as "egg millionaires" because by the time they are three months old, they release about a dozen ripe proglottids (egg envelopes) per day, each containing more than 100,000 eggs.

Usually, there is only one tapeworm living inside each host. That's because many tapeworms would damage the host—and if the host dies, so does the tapeworm.

Photo, facing page © SPL/Custom Medical Stock Photo

MICRO MONSTERS

INTESTINAL BLOOD FLUKE (*Schistosoma mansoni*)

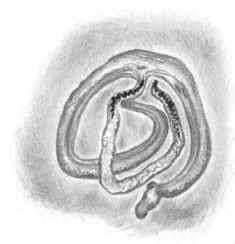

Blood flukes are parasites that live in the blood vessels of humans, their primary hosts. They cause the tropical illness schistosomiasis, an intestinal disease with flu-like symptoms. Different blood fluke species infect the bladder, the liver, and other organs in the human body. The intestinal blood fluke is found throughout Africa and in parts of South America and the West Indies.

Blood flukes always live as a pair; the threadlike female lies in the abdominal groove of the male. Fluke eggs make their way to the gut or bladder—causing much tissue damage—where they are eventually expelled. The larvae hatch in water and bore into their secondary host, a snail. After metamorphosis, they produce new larvae that swarm out of the snail and try to bore into a human host once again. People can only be infected in water, such as while swimming or working in irrigated fields. Once a larva has reached its human host, it is carried in the blood stream to the liver, where it matures.

Blood flukes are flatworms (so are tapeworms). Most flatworms are hermaphroditic, which means each one produces both eggs and sperm. Usually, they do not fertilize their own eggs.

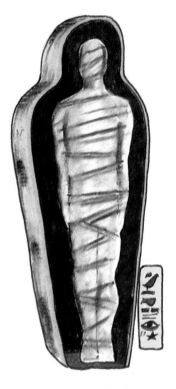

Health workers estimate that more than 100 million people are infected by blood flukes today. That's nothing new. Scientists know that ancient Egyptians suffered from the same parasite because they have discovered fluke eggs in mummies.

MICRO MONSTERS

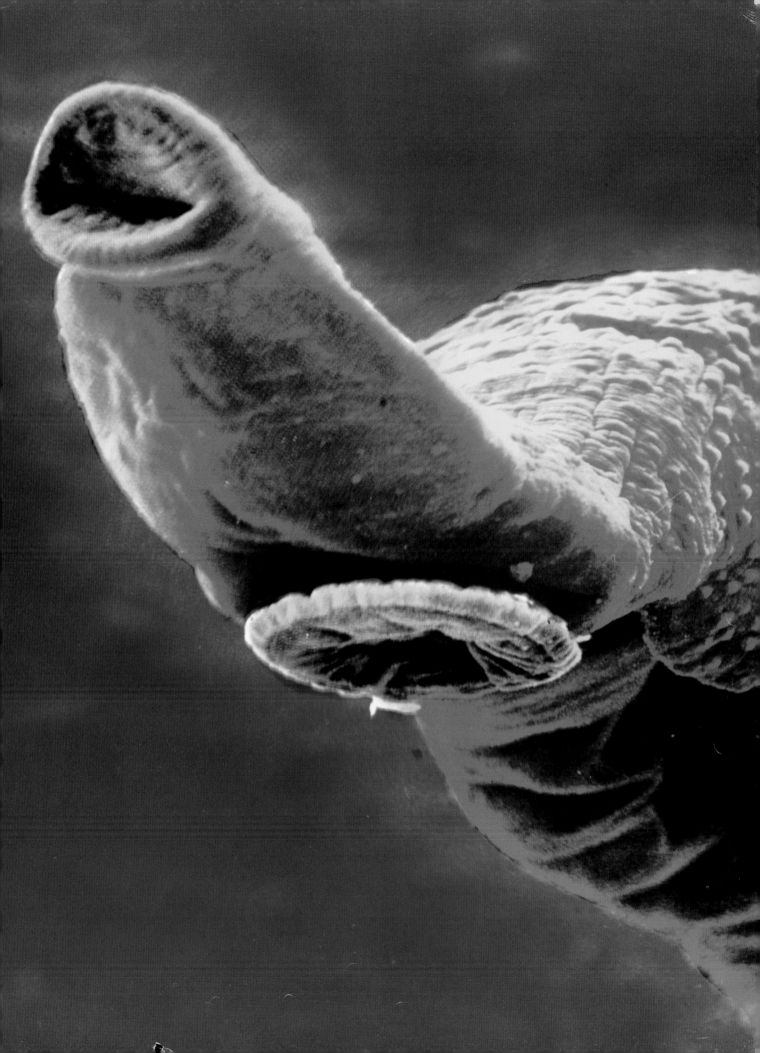

DUST MITE (*Glycyphagus* sp.)

Have you ever imagined alien life on distant planets? What about inside your household vacuum cleaner? Mighty tiny dust mites thrive in damp homes, and they munch on furniture. Furniture?! Yep. They also scavenge stuffing, wallpaper paste, groceries, and whatever else is handy. This particular dust mite uses its front, saw-toothed claws to collect flakes while browsing through a pile of skin cells, soil particles, and cat fur. Of course it looks monstrous—in the photo at right it has been magnified more than a hundred times—but it's usually harmless to humans.

Mites also live in rugs, pillows, and beds. Beware, about 2 million bed mites are found in the average mattress, and they might make you sneeze. Some folks are allergic to dust mites. Vacuuming bedding every day can ease your sneezes, not to mention your asthma.

Mites love to feed on skin cells. It sounds creepy, but remember that you shed millions of skin cells each day when you dress, scratch, brush, towel off, and toss and turn in bed.

Follicle mites are wormlike and they live head-down in the roots of some people's eyelashes. Eyelash mites use their eight clawed feet to get a grip. At night, when their host or hostess is sleeping, eyelash mites crawl out to find a mate or another resting place.

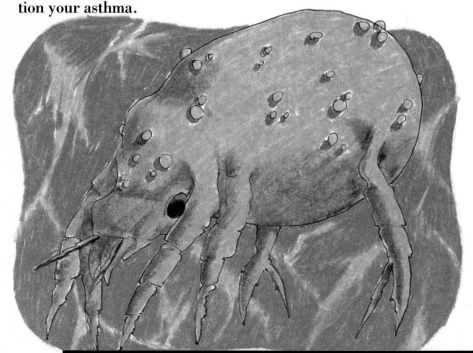

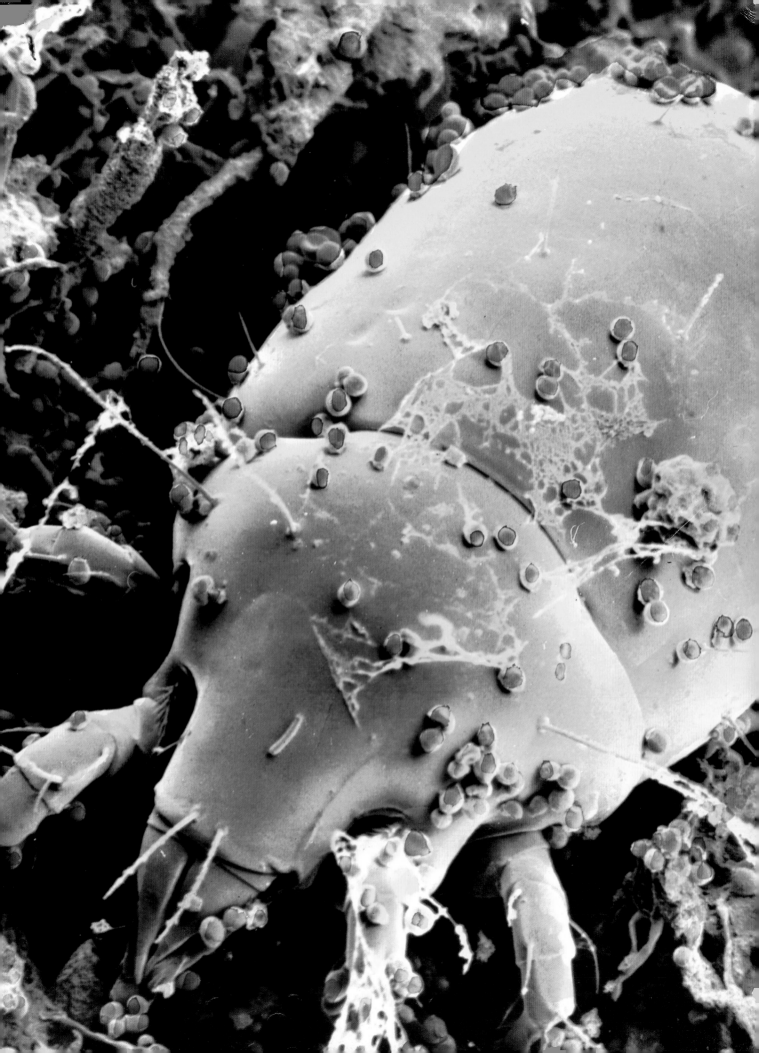

RED SPIDER MITE (Family: Tetranychidae)

There are roughly 10,000 species of mites, including plant and animal parasites. Red spider mites are plant parasites, and they live on vegetables, fruit trees, and flowers, which they cover with their fine webs. They feed mostly by sucking out the juices of leaf cells, and they cause the leaves to turn brownish-yellow and fall off.

Some species of mites—marine mites, for instance—have adapted to life underwater. These able swimmers are usually brightly colored predators, and they feed on other water animals. What do you think cheese mites eat? If you guessed cheese, you're only partly right. They also eat ham, sausage, and bacon.

All ticks and mites belong to the order Acarina. They have a one-piece, fused body. As adults they have eight legs, but in their larval stage they have only six legs.

Watch out for the human itch mite! This critter bores into skin and makes tunnels parallel to the surface. It causes itching, scabs, and blisters, especially on soft skin, such as between the fingers and under the arms.

Photo, facing page © Dr. Jeremy Burgess/SPL/Photo Researchers, Inc.

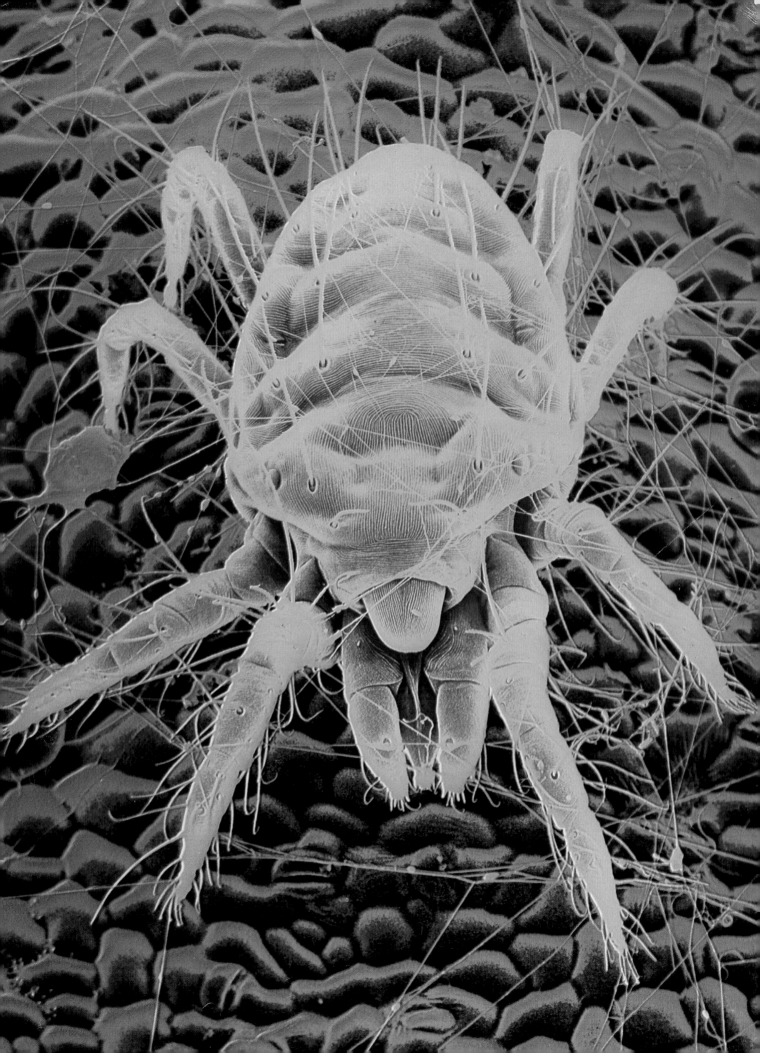

TARDIGRADE (*Macrobiotus* sp.)

Although they are commonly called water bears, tardigrades are tiny—usually between 0.1 and 1.0 millimeter long—cylinder-shaped animals. (When have you ever seen a bear that was a millimeter long?) Tardigrades sport four pair of stumpy legs that end in large claws, the better to grip slippery surfaces. They need to get a grip because they usually live in ditches, lakes, coastal waters, and in moist, mossy clumps growing on rocks.

The nifty tardigrade can survive for months in a dehydrated capsule state known as a "barrel." When conditions are right, the tardigrade returns to normal size and shape. When it comes to feeding, tardigrades use their two needlelike stylets to puncture a moss cell wall and suck out the contents. But they are not total vegetarians; they have been seen capturing and feeding on the bodies of other water critters, such as nematodes.

There are 300 to 400 known species of tardigrades. Because they are so tiny, tardigrades have no respiratory or circulatory organs.

The tardigrade at right has been magnified more than a hundred times. The long beanlike threads around it are algae.

Photo, facing page © Dr. Jeremy Burgess/SPL/Photo Researchers, Inc.

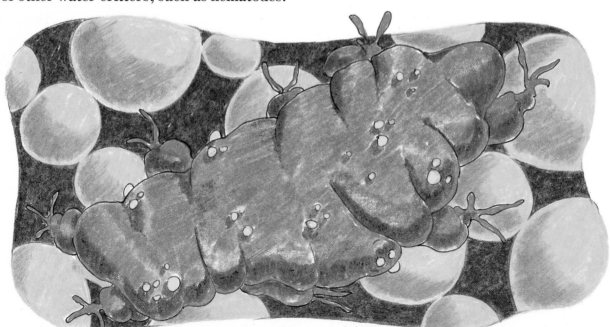

WOODWORM BEETLE (*Anobium punctatum*)

Furniture made of wood is the woodworm beetle's habitat of choice. In the larval stage, this minute critter nibbles and gnaws a path through tables, chairs, and desks. When the adult emerges from its burrow, it leaves behind a tell-tale trail of dry, powdery sawdust.

The female woodworm beetle crawls and flies around the room searching for the perfect piece of furniture, a nice woody spot on which to deposit her eggs.

Although woodworm beetles and other types of boring beetles are not harmful to humans, they can be expensive. Some species do millions of dollars' worth of damage boring into furniture, lumber, wine crates, and even bottle corks. Other species are strictly outdoor types. They live in dead wood and, sometimes, live trees.

Some collectors pay lots of money for antique furniture with beetle "worm holes." Hoping to make a buck, furniture makers have been known to drill their own woodworm beetle holes.

What's so special about a beetle? For one thing, a beetle boasts a pair of tough front wings (called elytra) that protect the delicate wings folded underneath. A beetle's skeleton is sturdier than that of many insects. And its primitive mouthparts are able to chew solid food, allowing it to prey on other animals.

Photo, facing page © Dr. Tony Brain/Photo Researchers, Inc.

DAPHNIA (*Daphnia pulex*)

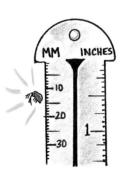

The daphnia, a tiny freshwater flea, is a crustacean. Crustaceans range in size from microscopic freshwater and saltwater fleas to large lobsters. Typically, they have a segmented body covered with plates of tough skin, or carapace, and two pairs of antennae. Water fleas do have a carapace that encloses their body but not their head, which projects below their beak.

Adult daphnias may reach a total length of .2 to 3 millimeters (0.008 to 0.12 inches).

Daphnia is the most common water flea to be found on the surface of lakes and ponds. It uses its sturdy, fringed antennae as oars to pull itself up and down through the water. (It can't move forward and back.) As it cruises, it sweeps microscopic algae into its mouth. Water fleas brood their young in a rear chamber of their body and commonly reproduce by parthenogenesis, which means the eggs are not fertilized by the male and develop into females only. Eventually, changes in temperature or food supply spur the production of eggs that produce males.

Daphnia and most other water fleas live in freshwater and filter tiny plant particles into their mouths. But a few marine water fleas are carnivores (meat-eaters). In turn, water fleas are a very important source of food for young fishes.

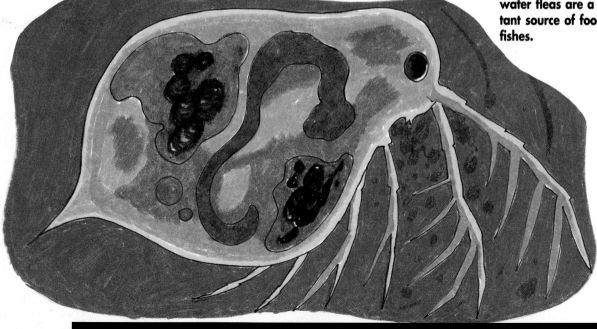

MAIZE WEEVIL (*Sitophilus granarius*)

When disturbed, adult weevils pretend they are dead.

Weevils are tiny beetles who have hard shells and extremely long snouts. Their eyes, elbowed antennae, and mouthparts are set very far apart from each other. The family known as true weevils (numbering at least 50,000 species) is the largest family in the entire animal kingdom. True weevils are sometimes called snout beetles, elephant beetles, and billbugs because most sport an extremely long proboscis, or snout.

True weevils, such as the maize weevil, are herbivores (they feed only on plants), and they live all over the world. They have a reputation for being pests because they often bore into wood, leaves, seeds, and other plant tissue. The maize weevil belongs to a group known as grain and rice weevils. The larvae bore and drill into the stems, seeds, and roots of plants and trees. Grain weevils feed on everything from farm crops to breakfast cereal.

Biting jaws at the very tip of the weevil's snout (rostrum) are used to chomp down; the snout itself is a drilling tool. The snout-weevil's antennae "elbow" out from either side of the snout. At each antenna's tip, a "hairy" club allows the weevil to sense the plant seed or stem surface into which it is drilling.

Photo, facing page © Dr. Tony Brain/SPL/Photo Researchers, Inc.

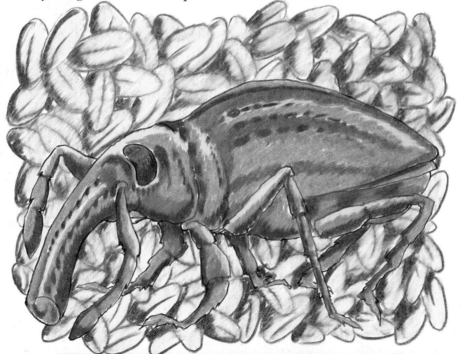

SPRINGTAIL (Order: Collembola)

The springtail is an extremely primitive insect; its fossil record dates back 300 million years. Today, there are about 1,500 species (it's no wonder the one at right is unidentified), and they all belong to the scientific order Collembola.

Springtails live in varied habitats, but most species prefer moist places. They feed on rotting plant or animal matter, and perhaps on algae and diatoms.

Some springtail species have a nifty habit of using their tails to spring into the air. This particular springtail (in the photo) sports no springing appendage because it lives below ground. It is pictured wandering through peat moss.

All springtails are wingless, and their eyes are primitive ocelli made up of six to eight light-sensitive cells. Most species are only a few millimeters or less in length.

The springtail at right has been magnified about 40 times. Like many of the photos in this book, this picture was taken with a scanning electron microscope (SEM). The image is produced by aiming a beam of electrons at the object or creature. The photographer then studies the resulting electron reflections on a special TV. This provides a vivid three-dimensional picture of the specimen.

Springtails are found all over the world, including in Arctic and Antarctic regions. One extremely unusual species of springtail, the snow flea, gathers in great numbers on top of snow, even on glacier snow fields.

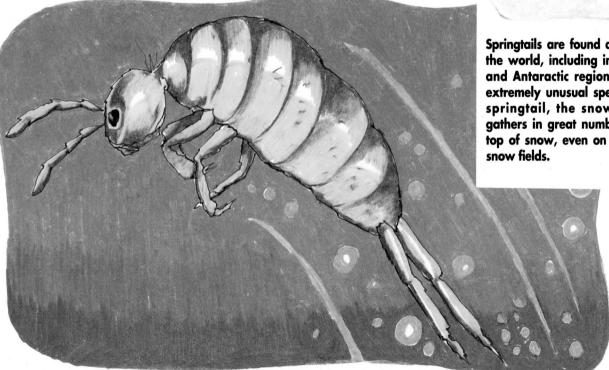

Photo, facing page © Dr. Jeremy Burgess/SPL/Photo Researchers, Inc.

MICRO MONSTERS

BEE LOUSE (*Braula coeca*)

The wingless bee louse is so tiny, it clings to the back of queen and drone honeybees and feeds directly from its host's mouth. As many as 180 bee lice can feed on a queen bee. While worker bees feed the queen, the louse sits on her head and sucks food right off her tongue. Like other parasites, the bee louse takes nourishment and shelter from its host without returning the favor.

Bee lice live in bee hives, where they deposit their eggs. After they hatch, bee louse larvae feed on the wax of the honeycomb that contains pollen. Scientists used to think there was only one species of bee louse, *Braula coeca*, which lives in Africa, Europe, and North and South America. Recently, however, they discovered a second species in Africa.

The wingless bee louse at right is resting on the back of a bee!

Many species of wingless flies die off because they can't escape their enemies or colonize new regions. However, one species of wingless fly is thriving on small, storm-swept islands in the Indian Ocean. It might not sound like a very nice place to live, but the violent winds destroy flying insects that would otherwise compete with the fly for food.

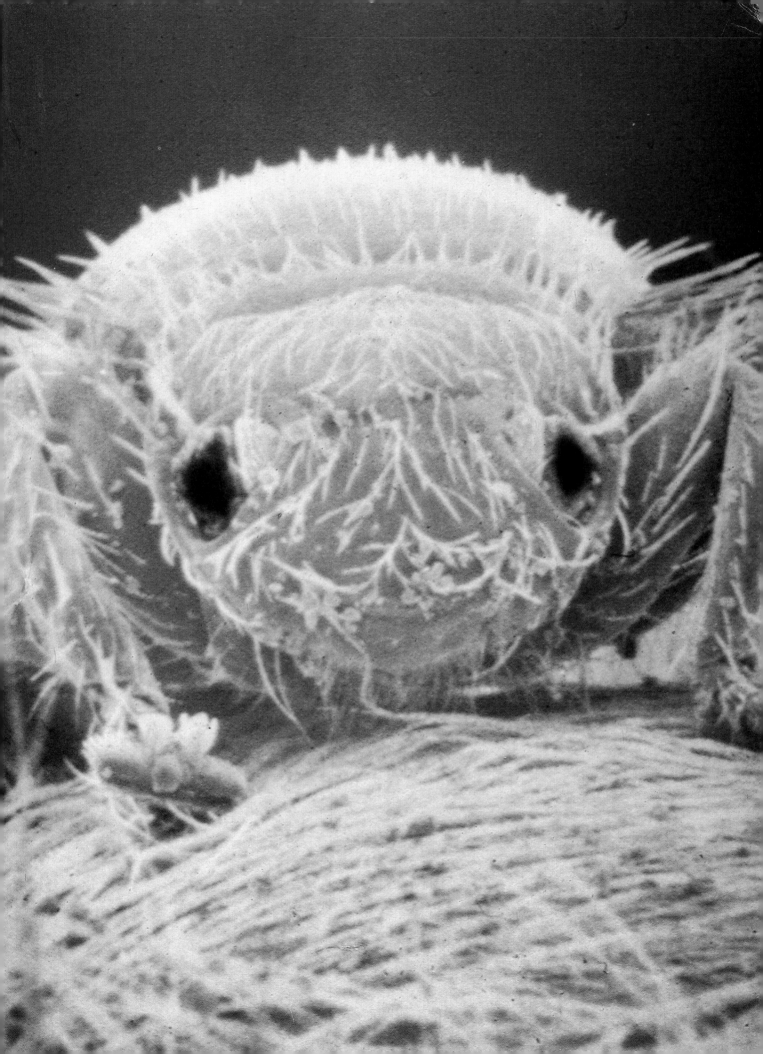

SHEEP KED (*Melophagus ovinus*)

The sheep ked is wingless, and for a long time it was mistaken for a tick. Actually it's a parasitic fly. By any name, the ked makes life a pain for domestic sheep and sheep farmers because it sucks the blood of the animals, causing skin irritation and lowering wool production.

Sheep ked larvae are retained in the adult female's body until they are almost fully matured. They are fed by the juices of special glands in the female. They then attach to the sheep's wool until they reach maturity. When fully grown, this parasite may reach a length of 6 millimeters (about $\frac{1}{4}$-inch).

Other louse flies live in the feathers of birds or in the fur of elk and deer, where they suck their host's blood. Many species of louse flies lose their wings when they settle on a host, but the sheep ked is wingless all its life.

Bat flies are blind, wingless louse flies that live on bats. When the bats roost in close quarters, the louse flies travel from one host to another with the greatest of ease.

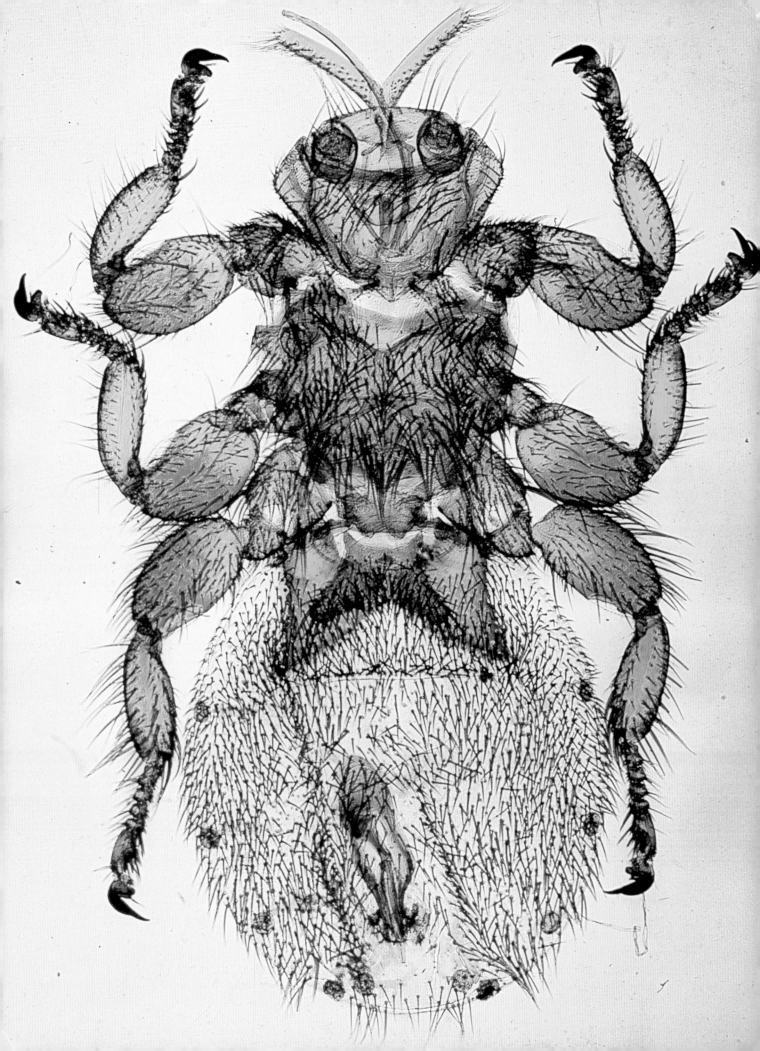

This glossarized index will help you find specific information about the micro monsters in this book. It will also help you understand the meaning of some of the words that are used.